Diego Mauricio Chiluisa Lagla

Teaching process of running technique in athletes from 10 to 11 years of age

AF155430

Diego Mauricio Chiluisa Lagla

Teaching process of running technique in athletes from 10 to 11 years of age

ScienciaScripts

This book is a translation from the original published under ISBN 978-620-3-03861-3.

Publisher:
Sciencia Scripts
is a trademark of
Dodo Books Indian Ocean Ltd. and OmniScriptum S.R.L publishing group

120 High Road, East Finchley, London, N2 9ED, United Kingdom
Str. Armeneasca 28/1, office 1, Chisinau MD-2012, Republic of Moldova, Europe
Managing Directors: Ieva Konstantinova, Victoria Ursu
info@omniscriptum.com

Printed at: see last page
ISBN: 978-620-3-52412-3

DEDICATÓRIA

This research work is dedicated in a special way to my mother who, thanks to her support at all times, made it possible for me to complete my studies.

The project is also dedicated to my family, aunts, uncles and grandparents because they have been present in every step I have taken, taking care of me and giving me strength to continue.

To my brother for his trust and unconditional support, who was also the one who had to accomplish this big step in one way or another.

To all the rest of my family and friends who have otherwise filled me with knowledge to be able to conclude a part of my studies.

THANK YOU

First I thank God for giving me wisdom, life and guiding me in each of the steps to accomplish one of my goals in life.

My undying gratitude to the Technical University of Ambato, to the Authorities and Teachers of the Faculty of Human Sciences and Education, to the Teachers of the Physical Culture Career, especially to Professor Raynier Montoro Bombú, thesis tutor, who with his professionalism and selflessness has guided me with his skills and knowledge in the development of my research, and therefore the satisfactory completion of this work.

Last but not least I would like to thank each and every one of the people who have been present in the realization of this project, I thank you from the bottom of my heart for having given me all the support, collaboration and encouragement but above all love and friendship.

INDEX

EXECUTIVE OVERVIEW

The present research work focuses on the teaching processes that lead to the learning of the running technique, for which an analysis of the problems of the research project and the current situation was carried out.

By means of the investigation it is intended to make a critical, reflexive and proactive evaluation about the teaching processes and methodologies, aimed at an adequate learning of the flat running technique, which through the application of the structured observation based on the technical evaluation sheet and at the same time making it participatory, The validity of each of the evaluated exercises of the technical card was checked by means of results based on the Student's test and the respective analysis and interpretation, this led us to the implementation of parameters that help the development and improvement of the technique, thus creating a guide of exercises.

Abstract

The present research work focuses on the teaching processes that lead to the learning of the career technique, by which an analysis of the research project problem and the current situation was carried out.

Through research, a critical, reflexive and proactive evaluation of the teaching processes and methodologies, aimed at an adequate learning of the technique of flat careers, which through the application of structured observation based on the research is intended Technical evaluation sheet and in turn making it participatory, it was verified by executing the practices based on the technical shortcomings and successes of the technique, for the validity of each of the evaluated exercises of the technical sheet were checked by results Based on the Student Test and the respective analysis and interpretation, this led us to the implementation of parameters that help the development and improvement of the technique, thus creating an exercise guide with the help of several training processes.

CHAPTER I

THEORETICAL FRAMEWORK

1.1 RESEARCH BACKGROUND

In order to deepen the theoretical component of the research, there are different antecedents and foundations related to the object of study. In this sense, through the method of review of documentary sources it was possible to verify the thesis of Cevallos Camacho (2014) in his research topic: Program of sports initiation in athletics to improve the teaching-learning processes in the students of the educational unit Machachi, Mejia canton, province of Pichincha, during the school year 2014-2015, in his research the author searches about the methodologies for teaching in the initiation of athletics, in turn concludes that: the didactic activities ludo techniques are valuable tools that allow to adequately guide the teaching-learning process of initiation to middle-distance athletics, in order to obtain new sports talents. The research work provides benefits to both athletes and coaches, because an innovative and adequate training method to improve technical fundamentals is made known. In turn (MOCHA-BONILLA, 2018) mentions that programmed activities should be planned through recreational games, i.e., carrying out activities with small games associated with the discipline of athletics.

Another of the atures consulted were Tobar & Zurata (2013) in their research topic: Methodological guide for the improvement of the running technique in long distance athletes of the Trotahacheros Club of the Municipality of Tuquerres - Narino, they report that a methodological guide for the improvement of the running technique in athletes allows improving the sports training processes, since from the scientific knowledge combined with the empirical knowledge is intended to achieve better sports performance. They also deduce that "the correct execution of the running technique contributes significantly to the sports result. They also mention that in long-distance running the correct technique is of great importance, since the rational displacement guarantees economy of movement and less energy expenditure.

According to (Narváez Galván, 2014) in his research topic: Pedagogical evaluation and its impact on competitive development in middle-distance events in pre-juvenile athletes of the Sports Federation of Loja period 2013; points out that when talking about pedagogical evaluation refers to a means that serves to check the teaching-learning process, so it takes into account the type of evaluation to apply according to the degree of efficiency in the competitive development in middle-distance events in order to avoid failure in the competitive development of the athlete. It also shows that the pedagogical controls do have a significant importance within the macro-planning carried out by the middle-distance coaches.

Teaching - Learning

The performance of the educator during the class applies a didactic technique according to a series of variables, which can be highlighted as the educational and teaching objectives to be achieved, the type of motor tasks to be taught, the characteristics of the students, etc.

The teaching technique aims at didactic communication, the educator's behaviors that are related to the way of giving information, the presentation of the tasks and activities to be performed by the student and all those reactions of the teacher to the performance and execution of the students. All those interventions of the teacher that are directly related to the transmission of skills and knowledge to the students are the object of the teaching technique.

The strategy in practice is the particular way of approaching the different exercises or tasks that make up the teaching progression of a given motor skill. The strategies in practice follow some of the ways of the thinking process such as synthesis and analysis, traditionally they have been known in didactics as the analytical method and the synthetic or global method.

The analytical strategy proceeds by decomposition or separation of the elements; the synthesis proceeds from the compound to the simple, composes the simple elements into the unit. The way to face the learning of many motor skills will depend on the complexity of it. (Sicilia Camacho & Delgado Noguera, 2002, p.23).

Sicilia Camacho et al. (2002) mention that "it is not possible to act in a fixed way in learning and teaching environments that are open. The most effective teaching styles are so to the extent that they most frequently produce the desired effects, but logically it is situational" (p.27).

Sbert, (1969) mentions that: "in order for a teacher to teach his students what he wants them to learn, it is necessary that he himself does certain things and that there are other things that must be done by the apprentices. It is not enough for them to see how the teacher does them, but the teacher must carefully formulate a work plan of the teacher's own activities and those that gradually correspond to the apprentices" (p.22).

Ortiz Ocana, (2009) refers to "learning as a **process of relatively permanent modification** of the student's mode of action that models and reshapes his experience according to the adaptation to the contexts in which the environment with which he relates, whether in the school or community, takes shape" (p.10).

García Cortina, (2018) explains that "learning is the faculty or ability that human beings have to understand things during the process of acquiring new habits and behaviors, it is significantly improved when the Self-structuring model of knowledge is applied, whose main attributes are: being objective, discrete, operant, optimistic, establishing proportion and concordance" (p.6).

"**Meaningful learning takes** place when students perceive the subject matter as relevant to their own purposes. Learning that involves a change in the organization of one's own ideas - in one's perception of oneself - is unsettling and tends to be resisted. The most useful socializing learning in the modern world is learning about the process of learning, an ongoing openness to experience and incorporate, in ourselves, the process of change. (Díaz Bordenave and Martins Pereira, 1997, p.57)

Athletics

Athletics is a sport composed of a set of skills and abilities, most of which come from natural human gestures, such as running, jumping or throwing. As a multidisciplinary sport, it has an enormous motor background that enhances its relevance in the educational sphere. The knowledge of the possibilities it offers, especially at the level of physical condition and in the field of coordination, should be a constant reference for Physical Education teachers. Athletics is structured on three of the basic skills in the motor behavior of the human being: displacements (running and walking), jumps and throws. (Hornillos Baz, 2000, p.5).

Athletics, the most natural of all sports, by its origins and by the characteristics of its exercises, corresponds to running also the most natural habit, since man acquires it from the first years of life. Whether for one reason or another, unfortunately, the habit formed in childhood is not the most appropriate, and the specialists in running, whether sprinting or long-distance, have to spend a lot of time correcting something that is strongly formed.

Sprint races are one of the most popular events. In this we can find the 100m, 200m, 100m hurdles, 400m hurdles and 400m flat. The 400m. flat race in all athletics events has been for a long time a point of attraction due to the biological characteristics that are performed in this sport modality. (Montoro, R, Hernández, V, Ortiz P, & Castro W, 2019).

The trainer must start from an accomplished fact: "all beginner athletes know how to run" and cannot forget that this is a natural ability and the beginner runs since the first years of life, when he abandoned the crawling and transformed his displacement in quadruped to bipedal form, however, he probably runs in an uneconomical and not very rational way, and the task of the trainer is to transform a habit that, in a natural way, has been badly formed. The methodology of teaching the technique of flat running should be governed by the principle of transforming the natural into the rational. (Romero Frometa and Scrubb, 2003).

Running technique

Vinuesa (1997) points out that "running, the classic athletic sport, can be considered both simple and difficult; simple because it is a natural ability that everyone, even the less gifted, performs at some time in their lives" (p.14).

So it is necessary to mention that running technique is the way we have to execute the movements involved in the gesture of running, a good running technique would be the model that a runner can perform in the gait cycle from the biomechanical, motor and energetic point of view. A good running technique can not only make the difference between running with or without pain, but it also helps to improve your performance. (School of RUNNING, 2019)

Benefits

- Reduces the risk of suffering any type of injury.

- Achieve higher speed and improve performance.

- To save as much energy as possible while training.

- Delay the onset of muscle fatigue as much as possible.

- Increase agility and body coordination.

- Improve the efficiency of movements.

- Acquire a more comfortable and elegant running posture.

Brigaud (2015) mentions that "the development of the ability to maintain the organization of the body in the technical sporting gesture should be the starting point of any activity for the purpose of optimization and preservation. It should not be omitted that maintaining a posture entails an additional energetic cost, but the performance obtained is superior" (p.3)

The position

Posture is understood to be the variations in the positioning of some parts of the body in relation to others, as well as their ability to maintain them in spite of tensions. Ability to maintain an efficient and physiological positioning of the different parts of the body (Brigaud, 2015).

Good posture starts from head to toe: eyes, neck, shoulders, arms, hands, back, hips, legs, knees and feet.

In practice it is necessary to try to apply two aspects such as the demonstration of the test in full, and the explanation of the technical aspects simultaneously, and then demonstrate the complete movement at different speeds and also the same coach is explaining the most important aspects. Remember that at this age children need more of the demonstration than the explanation.

As is unquestionable, the athlete will perform it incorrectly, with an inadequate technique. No matter, this first confrontation with the complete movement is very important for him: it will offer him his first conscious motor experience of the technique he is going to learn and, most importantly, it will motivate him to learn the fractional movement.

For a correct management of teaching and learning, 2 principles of training are applied such as the principle of individualization due to the fact that no athlete is equal to the other so it does not make sense to have the same training plan for everyone, on the other hand is the principle of specificity which tries to improve each aspect in the sport, consequently to the subject of study we are dealing with the running technique.

Now starting from the fact that the teaching of athletics is directed towards four fundamental areas that group characteristic tests for their execution, within these we can find the walk or sport march, the races, the jumps and the throws. In all these tests, a wide range of contents are taught, allowing students to deepen their knowledge of this sport. Taking into account the speed with which the current context is developing and the scarce theoretical preparation shown by novice teachers during the teaching process, it is necessary to continue deepening the teaching of the technical fundamentals that support the development of athletics in its current context. (Montoro, Quizhpe, Ochoa & Medina; 2018). In this sense, the general objective of the research is stated.

1.2 OBJECTIVES

General Objective

- To establish adjustments in the teaching process of the running technique that will allow a correct performance of the flat running technique.

Specific objectives

- To analyze the theoretical and methodological references that support the study of the current state of the teaching-learning process of the running technique of the child athletes of the Tungurahua Sports Federation.

- To examine the teaching-learning processes of the running technique applied to child athletes of the Tungurahua Sports Federation.

- To design an exercise guide for the improvement of the running technique in athletes from 10 to 11 years old of the Tungurahua Sports Federation.

To establish adjustments in the teaching process of the running technique that allows a correct performance of the flat running technique. After the analysis and examination of the teaching-learning processes of the running technique, a methodological guide was used for an adequate practice of this skill to be improved, the first step to be taken into account was the identification of the need to improve within the running technique based on the parameters to be evaluated such as trunk posture, hip, braking, the look, the position of the hands, the movement of the lower limbs, being these fundamental aspects in competition, then we move to the next step which is the determination to establish new adjustments to the training guide therefore this point was explicit by the researcher in this case my person for a new approach which will help the improvement in child athletes, then proceeded to the request or the corresponding approval by the coach or trainers in charge which were first taken into consideration to implement new adjustments to their training plan, then proceeded to review the exercises to apply, to immediately proceed to the approval of the same, then went to the implementation of the adjustments which were both the responsibility of both the researcher and the coaches and the institution itself, In addition, the corresponding observation was made together with the evaluation card to represent a correct development in the improvement of the running technique, as a last step, a follow-up was made with the objective of seeing the athlete developing the running technique adequately within the flat races in the established time of the research.

In this way, the corresponding practices were coordinated with the established exercises, which were given progressively, depending on each of the movements to be strengthened in the practices carried out with the child athletes. This was carried out through experimentation and observation, by establishing with the help of the coach and myself several exercises that the child athletes had to perform, noting the improvement that is occurring in terms of the development of this feature, basic exercises were applied, reaching the execution of exercises with greater complexity for these ages.

To analyze the theoretical and methodological references that support the study of the current state of the teaching-learning process of the running technique of child athletes of the Tungurahua Sports Federation. The respective collection of existing substantial knowledge on the research topic was carried out and used as a basis for the initiation, development and completion of the research work, these theoretical references were of utmost importance for the approach of exercises that help the development of the running technique and therefore the creation of the methodological guide, as well as for the approach and interpretation of the results obtained. It should be emphasized that all this background was investigated in scientific articles that focus on the collection of scientific truthful information on the aforementioned topic, books, the repository of the Technical University of Ambato as well as other universities inside and outside the country and last but not least reliable websites were also investigated.

To examine the teaching-learning processes of the running technique applied to the children athletes of the Tungurahua Sports Federation. For the exploration of the teaching and learning processes we proceeded with the execution of the corresponding practices by the coach and the athletes, the first step to examine was the teaching process which is the most important task of the coach which consists of accompanying the athlete's learning, as main characteristic we examined the content and the application of the techniques to teach, after this we went to the learning process which is the responsibility of the athlete in this case, with the guidance of the coach we observed how he/she carries out an adequate development of the running technique.

In this way, the teaching processes applied to the learning of the running technique of child athletes were examined. This activity was carried out by means of a correctly structured observation for the collection of information, which was essential to proceed to the next step that leads to the establishment of adjustments for the development of the running technique in flat races.

To design a guide of exercises for the improvement of the running technique in athletes from 10 to 11 years old of the Tungurahua Sports Federation. For the fulfillment of this objective we had the appropriate means for the corresponding practice and evaluation such as the athletic track, the means of observation which in this case was the technical evaluation card, a video camera, we also had the support of the same coaches of the discipline of athletics as well as the indispensable support of the athletes, Consequently, we proceeded with the fulfillment of the specific objectives which are characterized by the analysis of the theoretical and methodological references, the examination of the teaching-learning processes in terms of the running technique, and adjustments were established according to the training program for the improvement of this characteristic.

We know that the exercise guide is a fundamental tool in the process of autonomous learning, so as a first step towards the realization of the guide, the necessary information that demonstrates the validity, quality and updating of the designed tool was recorded. Next, the elements to be included in the methodological planning were defined, and finally the plan of activities, in this case the plan of exercises according to each one of the parameters to be taken into account in the running technique.

CHAPTER II

METHODOLOGY

MATERIALS

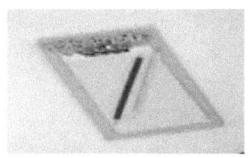

Table of annotations

Laptop

Prints

Athletic track

Cones

Whistle

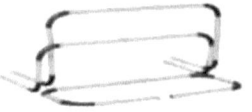   

| Fences | Cellular |

Graph 1 Materials

2.2 METHODS

The research topic called: Current state of the teaching-learning process of the running technique of the 10 to 11 years old athletes of the F.D.T. is aimed at the formulation of new training processes through the support of an exercise guide, which is efficient in the teaching-learning stage of child athletes.

Approach

The project by the characteristics of the elements to investigate and for the formulation of the solutions a quantitative and qualitative approach was used by the fact of the analysis of the reality of coaches and athletes in terms of teaching and learning, referring to the quantitative pattern this allowed to demonstrate numerical data generated in tabulations of the survey, and the same observation which has parameters to evaluate the technique of child athletes of the Sports Federation of Tungurahua. In addition, the scientific method was used to obtain theoretical knowledge with validity and scientific verification through the use of reliable instruments, such as surveys and observation.

Research processes used.

The present research work is bibliographic documentary, because it allowed to analyze, synthesize, expand or compare different points of view of several authors, theories, criteria and topics related to the teaching-learning processes in the running technique. It is also based on field research because it was carried out in the place of the facts where we worked with the coaches and athletes of the F.D.T.

For the empirical inquiries, other methods were used such as: the review of official documents, which allowed to consult among other writings; the degree theses of different universities in the country, and theses of universities in Latin America. All this was used in the search for information establishing a level of satisfaction about the methodical development in the career technique. In addition, based on the observation method, through a technical card we were able to obtain data on the impact of the teaching-learning programs on the improvement of the running technique of athletes from 10 to 11 years of age of the Tungurahua Sports Federation.

Sample

The research sample is based on the discipline studied and the ages of 10 to 11 years so we will have a sample n-12 athletes of a total population n-12 athletes who are permanently training in the facilities of the Sports Federation of Tungurahua. In addition there were 3 coaches giving a total of 15 involved within the F.D.T.

Procedure

For the correct development of the teaching-learning processes based on the running technique, we resorted to the observation with the execution of four basic but essential exercises called SPRINT, in order to equalize the progress, they were shaped in 5 weeks. In the first week we performed the running exercise lifting thighs, which had the objective of establishing the runner the habit of lifting knees. The second week we performed the running exercise lifting thighs with extension of the legs in front, which had the objective of increasing the length of the stride. In the third week, the exercise called running with extension of the lower extremities was performed, the objective of which was the rapid descent of the lower extremities. In week 4, the exercise of running 50 was performed, the objective of which was to contribute to the improvement of the coordination of the lower and upper extremities.

At the end of week 5, the respective evaluation of the running technique was carried out with the established parameters. It should be emphasized that in each of the exercises, fundamental parameters such as position of the upper limbs, position of the trunk, hips, as well as the improvement of coordination, concentration and relaxation of the athletes were observed, all these aspects were raised in the observation sheet. The methodological process was carried out with the respective observation that had as objective the identification of data on the facts in the running technique. Then we proceeded to the tabulation of results and the verification with the help of the Shapiro-will statistical test to determine the levels of reliability by means of Student's t-test, the application of this test was given by the fact of calculating related samples and having a small sample of less than 30 individuals. Subsequently, a teaching guide for the running technique was elaborated, which allowed a correct performance of the flat running technique.

Table of indicators to be evaluated by work weeks.

TECHNICAL EVALUATION SHEET		
Evaluation of four technical running exercises, each with 8 parameters to be evaluated with a score from 1 to 4, 4 being the highest score.		
Name:		
Parameters	**Pre**	**Pos**
Running with thigh lift Distance: 20 - 30 m.		
Fluid movement without excessive contraction of the muscle planes.		
2. Front view		
3. Angle of 90° in the swing and not to go beyond the centerline of the body.		
4. Semi-closed hands		
5. Upright trunk		
6. High hips		
7. The elevated leg must be parallel to the ground with the knee bent at a 90° angle, toe facing forward.		
8. Supporting leg fully extended and resting on the metatarsal.		
Thigh lift run with leg extension in front Distance: 20 - 30 m.		
Fluid movement without excessive contraction of the muscle planes.		
2. Front view		
3. Angle of 90° in the swing and not to go beyond the centerline of the body.		
4. Semi-closed hands		
5. Upright trunk		
6. High hips		
7. The elevated leg then picked up shall be extended and parallel to the ground with the toe of the foot slightly bent forward.		
8. Supporting leg extended and resting on the metatarsal.		
Running with extension of the lower extremities		
Fluid movement without excessive contraction of the muscle planes.		
2. Front view		
3. Angle of 90° in the swing and not to go beyond the centerline of the body.		
4. Semi-closed hands		
5. Upright trunk		
6. High hips		
7. The elevated leg shall be extended at a 45° angle to the other, the toe of the foot slightly bent forward.		
8. Supporting leg extended and resting on the metatarsal.		

50 m race		
Fluid movement without excessive contraction of the muscle planes.		
2. Front view		
3. Angle of 90° in the swing and not to go beyond the centerline of the body.		
4. Semi-closed hands		
5. Upright trunk		
6. High hips		
7. Coordination between upper and lower extremities.		
8. Supporting leg extended and resting on the metatarsal.		

Prepared by: (Montoro., 2013)

CHAPTER III

RESULTS AND DISCUSSION

3.1 ANALYSIS AND DISCUSSION OF RESULTS

Research results

After the application of the observation and therefore the respective evaluation form with the post and pre-test, the results were tabulated, taking into account the results obtained in each of the evaluated parameters. The alternative results were taken into account, establishing in each one of them the frequency or repetition of the information.

The results of the research presented in this chapter are related to the variables of the subject, which allowed the development of the research instruments, to be subsequently applied to the entire universe of work.

From the tabulation of data, statistical tables and comparative graphs were designed, which contain percentages based on the results of the work universe, for each of the exercises and parameters proposed for each of the variables. The information obtained is organized in such a way that it responds to the objectives set out in the research.

Running with thigh lift

	Pre test				
	1				Total
1.	0				1
2.	0				0
3.	0		5		0
4.	1				1
5.	0		0		1
6.	0		0		
7.	0				0
8.	0			5	5

Table 1 Running with thigh raises Pre test

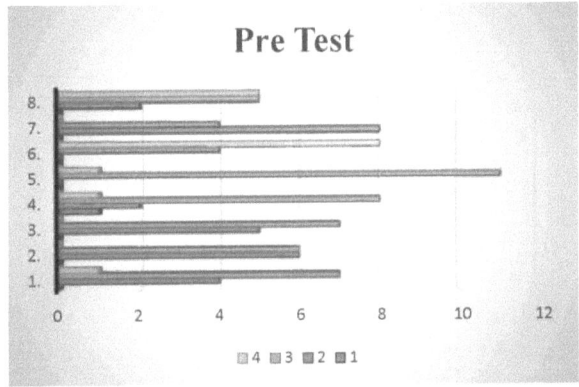

Figure 2 Running with thigh raise Pre test

Table 1: shows the results of the observations of the race with thigh lift in the pre-test, there are 8 evaluated parameters, from 1 to 4 being 1 the lowest qualification and 4 the highest qualification, therefore in parameter 1, 4 athletes have the qualification of 2, 7 athletes with qualification of 3 and 1 athlete with qualification of 4 giving us a total of 12 evaluated athletes. in parameter 2, 6 athletes have the qualification of 2, and 6 athletes with qualification of 3 giving us a total of 12 evaluated athletes. In parameter 3, 5 athletes have the qualification of 2, and 7 athletes with qualification of 3 giving us a total of 12 evaluated athletes. In parameter 4, one athlete has the qualification of 1, 2 athletes have the qualification of 2, 8 athletes with qualification of 3 and 1 athlete with qualification of 4 giving us a total of 12 evaluated athletes. In parameter 5, 11 athletes have the qualification of 3 and 1 athlete with qualification of 4 giving us a total of 12 evaluated athletes. In parameter 6, 4 athletes have the qualification of 3 and 8 athletes have the qualification of 4 giving us a total of 12 evaluated athletes. In parameter 7, 8 athletes have the qualification of 2, 4 athletes have the qualification of 3 giving us a total of 12 evaluated athletes. In parameter 8, 2 athletes have a score of 2, 5 athletes have a score of 3 and 5 athletes have a score of 4 giving us a total of 12 evaluated athletes.

Thigh lift run with front leg extension

			're test		
	1				Total
1.	0				1
2.	0	5			0
3.	0				0
4.	1				1
5.	0	0			0
6.	0	0			
7.	0		1		1
8.	0				

Table 2 Thigh lift run with forward leg extension Pre test

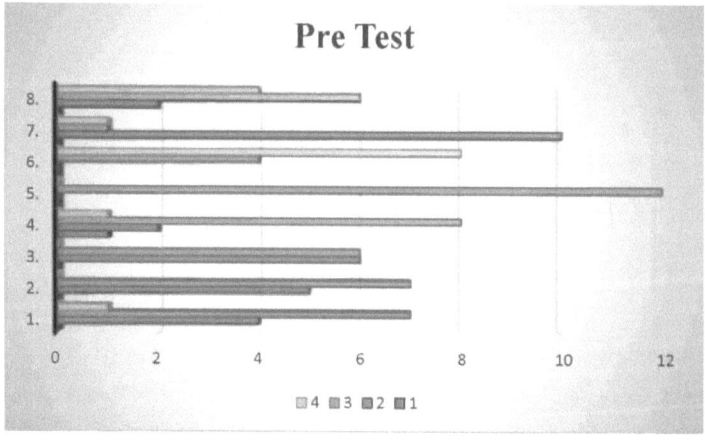

Figure 3 Thigh lift run with forward leg extension Pre test

Table 2: shows the results of the observations of the race lifting thighs with front leg extension in the pre-test, there are 8 evaluated parameters, from 1 to 4 being this the highest qualification, therefore in parameter 1, 4 athletes have the qualification of 2, 7 athletes with qualification of 3 and only 1 athlete with qualification of 4 giving us a total of 12 evaluated athletes. In parameter 2, 5 athletes have the qualification of 2, and 7 athletes with qualification of 3 giving us a total of 12 evaluated athletes. In parameter 3, 6 athletes have the qualification of 2, and 6 athletes with qualification of 3 giving us a total of 12 evaluated athletes. In parameter 4, one athlete has a score of 1, 2 athletes have a score of 2, 8 athletes have a score of 3 and 1 athlete has a score of 4 giving us a total of 12 athletes evaluated. In parameter 5, 12 athletes have a score of 3 giving us a total of 12 athletes evaluated. In parameter 6, 4 athletes have the qualification of 3 and 8 athletes have the qualification of 4 giving us a total of 12 evaluated athletes. In parameter 7, 10 athletes have the qualification of 2, one athlete the qualification of 3 and 1 athlete the qualification of 4 giving us a total of 12 evaluated athletes. In parameter 8, 2 athletes have a score of 2, 6 athletes with a score of 3 and 4 athletes with a score of 4 giving us a total of 12 evaluated athletes.

Running with extension of the lower extremities

	Pre test				
	1				Total
1.	0				1
2.	0	5			0
3.	0				0
4.	1				1
5.	0	0			
6.	0	0			
7.	0	0	1		
8.	0	0			

Table 3 Running with lower limb extension Pre test

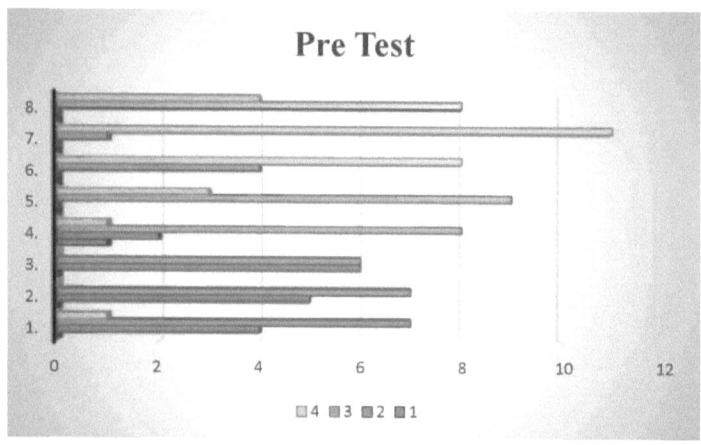

Figure 4 Running with lower limb extension Pre test

Table 3: shows the results of the observations of the running with extension of the lower extremities in the pre-test, there are 8 evaluated parameters, from 1 to 4 being this the highest qualification, therefore in parameter 1, 4 athletes have the qualification of 2, 7 athletes with qualification of 3 and only 1 athlete with qualification of 4 giving us a total of 12 evaluated athletes. In parameter 2, 5 athletes have the qualification of 2, and 7 athletes with qualification of 3 giving us a total of 12 evaluated athletes. In parameter 3, 6 athletes have the qualification of 2, and 6 athletes with qualification of 3 giving us a total of 12 evaluated athletes. In parameter 4, one athlete has a score of 1, 2 athletes have a score of 2, 8 athletes have a score of 3 and 1 athlete has a score of 4 giving us a total of 12 athletes evaluated. In parameter 5, 9 athletes have a score of 3 and 3 athletes have a score of 4 giving us a total of 12 athletes evaluated. In parameter 6, one athlete has the qualification of 3 and 11 athletes have the qualification of 4 giving us a total of 12 evaluated athletes. In parameter 7, 4 athletes have the qualification of 2, and 8 athletes have the qualification of 3 giving us a total of 12 evaluated athletes. In parameter 8, 4 athletes have a score of 3 and 8 athletes have a score of 4, giving us a total of 12 evaluated athletes.

50 m race

	Pre test				
	1				Total
1.	0				
2.	0	5			0
3.	0				0
4.	1	0			1
5.	0	0			
6.	0	0		1	
7.	0	0			
8.	0	1	5		

Table 4 50 m race Pre test

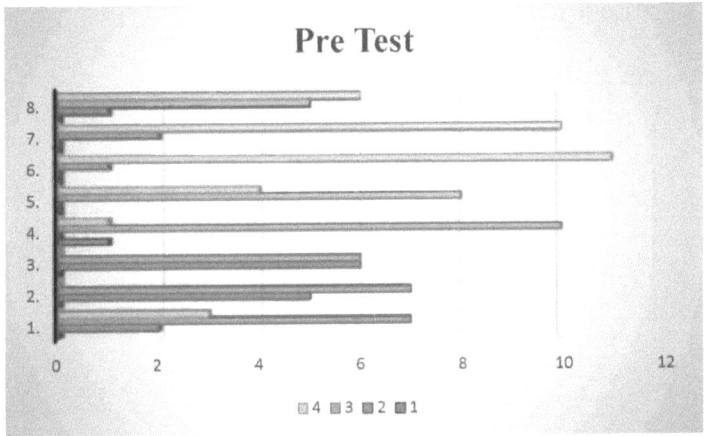

Figure 5 50 m race Pre test

Table 4: shows the results of the observations of the 50 m. race in the pre-test, there are 8 evaluated parameters, from 1 to 4 being this the highest qualification, therefore in parameter 1, 2 athletes have the qualification of 2, 7 athletes with qualification of 3 and 3 athletes with qualification of 4 giving us a total of 12 evaluated athletes. In parameter 2, 5 athletes have the qualification of 2, and 7 athletes with qualification of 3 giving us a total of 12 evaluated athletes. In parameter 3, 6 athletes have the qualification of 2, and 6 athletes with qualification of 3 giving us a total of 12 evaluated athletes. In parameter 4, one athlete has the qualification of 1, 10 athletes have the qualification of 3, one athlete has the qualification of 4 giving us a total of 12 evaluated athletes. In parameter 5, 8 athletes have a score of 3 and 4 athletes have a score of

4 giving us a total of 12 athletes evaluated. In parameter 6, one athlete has the qualification of 3 and 11 athletes have the qualification of 4 giving us a total of 12 evaluated athletes. In parameter 7, 2 athletes have the qualification of 3, and 10 athletes have the qualification of 4 giving us a total of 12 evaluated athletes. In parameter 8, one athlete has a score of 2, 5 athletes have a score of 3 and 6 athletes have a score of 4 giving us a total of 12 athletes evaluated.

Analysis of post-test results

Running with thigh lift

	Pos	test		
	1			Total
1.	0	1		
2.	0	1		
3.	0	0		
4.	0	0		
5.	0	0		
6.	0	0	0	
7.	0	0		
8.	0	0		

Table 5 Running with thigh raises Post test

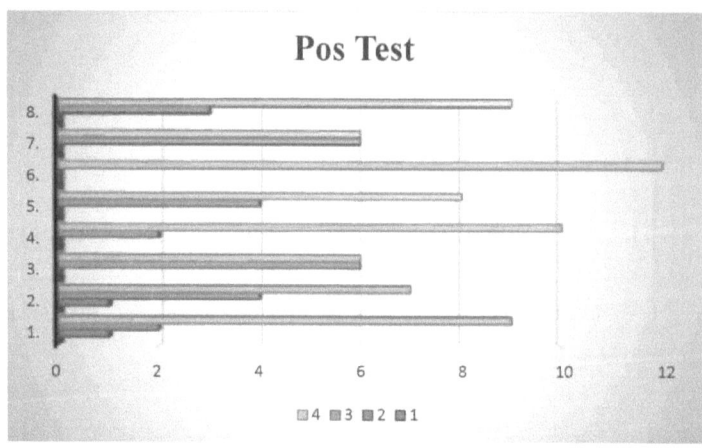

Figure 6 Running with thigh lift Post test

Table 5: shows the results of the observations of the thigh lift running in the post test, there are 8 evaluated parameters, from 1 to 4 being this the highest qualification, therefore in parameter 1, one athlete has the qualification of 2, 2 athletes have the qualification of 3, and 9 athletes with qualification of 4 giving us a total of 12 evaluated athletes. In parameter 2, one athlete has the qualification of 2, 4 athletes have the qualification of 3 and 7 athletes have the qualification of 4 giving us a total of 12 evaluated athletes. In parameter 3, 6 athletes have the qualification of 3, and 6 athletes with qualification of 4 giving us a total of 12 evaluated athletes. In parameter 4, 2 athletes have the qualification of 3, and 10 athletes have the qualification of 4, giving us a total of 12 evaluated athletes. In parameter 5, 4 athletes have the qualification of 3 and 8 athletes have the qualification of 4 giving us a total of 12 evaluated athletes. In parameter 6, 12 athletes have a score of 4 with a total of 12 athletes evaluated. In parameter 7, 6 athletes have the qualification of 3, and 6 athletes have the qualification of 4 giving us a total of 12 evaluated athletes. In parameter 8, 3 athletes have the qualification of 3, and 9 athletes have the qualification of 4 giving us a total of 12 evaluated athletes. As can be observed

Thigh lift run with leg extension with legs out in front

	Post test				
	1				Total
1.	0	0			
2.	0	1			
3.	0	0			
4.	0	0			
5.	0	0	5		
6.	0	0	0		
7.	0	0			
8.	0	0			

Table 6 Thigh lift run with forward leg extension Post test

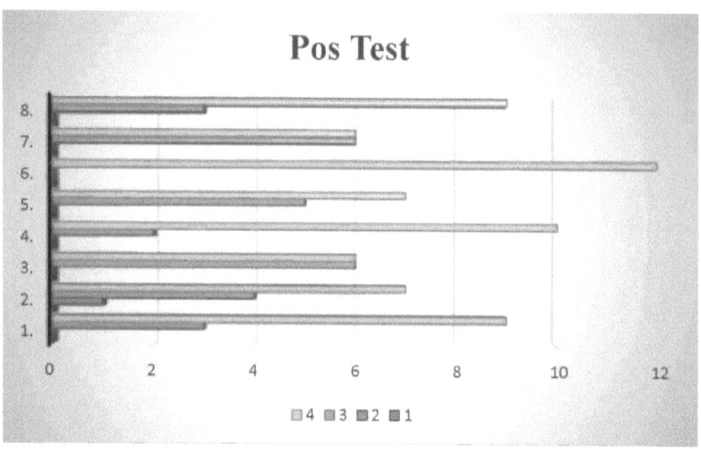

Figure 7 Thigh lift run with forward leg extension Post test

Table 6: shows the results of the observations of the thigh lifting run with leg extension to the front in the post test, there are 8 evaluated parameters, from 1 to 4 being this the highest qualification, therefore in parameter 1, 2 athletes have the qualification of 3, and 10 athletes with qualification of 4 giving us a total of 12 evaluated athletes. In parameter 2, one athlete has the qualification of 2, 4 athletes with qualification of 3 and 7 athletes with qualification of 4 giving us a total of 12 evaluated athletes. In parameter 3, 6 athletes have the qualification of 3, and 6 athletes with qualification of 4 giving us a total of 12 evaluated athletes. In parameter 4, 2 athletes have the qualification of 3, and 10 athletes have the qualification of 4, giving us a total of 12 evaluated athletes. In parameter 5, 5 athletes have the qualification of 3 and 7 athletes have the qualification of 4 giving us a total of 12 evaluated athletes. In parameter 6, 12 athletes have a score of 4 with a total of 12 athletes evaluated. In parameter 7, 6 athletes have the qualification of 3, and 6 athletes have the qualification of 4 giving us a total of 12 evaluated athletes. In parameter 8, 3 athletes have the qualification of 3, and 9 athletes have the qualification of 4 giving us a total of 12 evaluated athletes.

Running with lower limb extension

	Post test					
	1				Total	
1.	0	0				
2.	0	1	5			
3.	0	0				
4.	0	0				
5.	0	0	0			
6.	0	0	0			
7.	0	0				
8.	0	0	1			

Table 7 Running with lower limb extension Post test

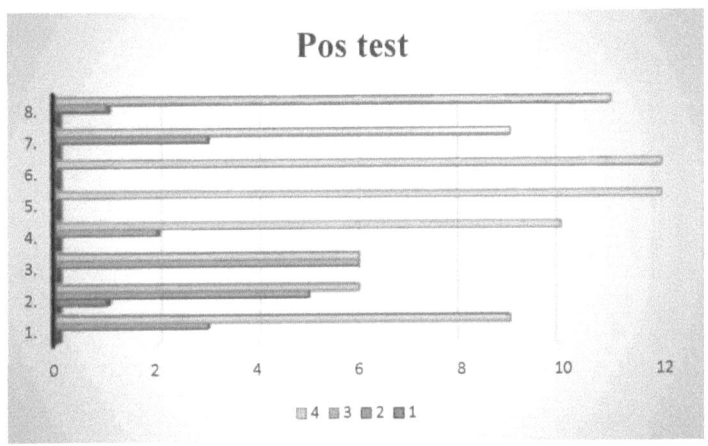

Figure 8 Running with lower limb extension Post test

Table 7: shows the results of the observations of the Running with extension of the lower extremities in the post-test, there are 8 evaluated parameters, from 1 to 4 being this the highest qualification, therefore in parameter 1, 3 athletes have the qualification of 3, and 9 athletes with qualification of 4 giving us a total of 12 evaluated athletes. In parameter 2, one athlete has the qualification of 2, 5 athletes with qualification of 3 and 6 athletes with qualification of 4 giving us a total of 12 evaluated athletes. In parameter 3, 6 athletes have the qualification of 3, and 6 athletes with qualification of 4 giving us a total of 12 evaluated athletes. In parameter 4, 2 athletes have the qualification of 3, and 10 athletes have the qualification of 4, giving us a total of 12 evaluated athletes. In parameter 5, 12 athletes have a score of 4 with a total of 12 athletes evaluated. In parameter 6, 12 athletes have a score of 4 with a total of 12 athletes evaluated. In parameter 7, 3 athletes have the qualification of 3, and 9 athletes have the qualification of 4 giving us a total of 12 evaluated athletes. In parameter 8, one athlete has a score of 3, and 11 athletes have a score of 4 giving us a total of 12 athletes evaluated.

50 m race.

	Post test				
	1				Total
1.	0	0			
2.	0	1	5		
3.	0	0			
4.	0	0	1		
5.	0	0	0		
6.	0	0	0		
7.	0	0	0		
8.	0	0	1		

Table 8 50 m race Post test

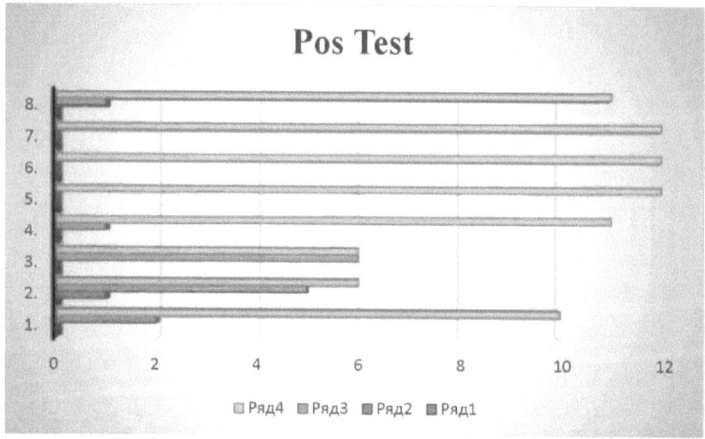

Figure 9 50 m race Post test

Table 7: shows the results of the observations of the 50m race in the post test, there are 8 evaluated parameters, from 1 to 4 being this the highest qualification, therefore in parameter 1, 2 athletes have the qualification of 3, and 10 athletes with qualification of 4 giving us a total of 12 evaluated athletes. In parameter 2, one athlete has the qualification of 2, 5 athletes with qualification of 3 and 6 athletes with qualification of 4 giving us a total of 12 evaluated athletes. In parameter 3, 6 athletes have the qualification of 3, and 6 athletes with qualification of 4 giving us a total of 12 evaluated athletes. In parameter 4, one athlete has the qualification of 3, and 11 athletes have the qualification of 4, giving us a total of 12 evaluated athletes. In parameter 5, 12 athletes have a score of 4 with a total of 12 athletes evaluated. In parameter 6, 12 athletes have a score of 4 with a total of 12 athletes evaluated. In parameter 7, 12 athletes have a score of 4 with a total of 12 athletes evaluated. In parameter 8, one athlete has a score of 3, and 11 athletes have a score of 4 giving us a total of 12 athletes evaluated.

STATISTICAL TESTING

T STUDENT

Hypothesis

Ho: There is no significant difference between pre-test and post-test of running technique.

H1: There is a significant difference between pre-test and post-test of running technique.

ALPHA ": 0.05

Running with thigh lift

Normality

Kolmogorov - Smirnov: for large samples (> 30 individuals)

Shapiro - Wilk: small samples (< 30 individuals)

Criteria for determining normality:

Pre test => a = 0.05 Ho = The data come from a normal distribution.

Pos test < a = 0.05 H1 = The data do not come from a normal distribution.

Case processing summary

33

	Cases					
	Valid		Lost		Total	
	N	Percentage	N	Percentage	N	Percentage
Pre test		100,0%	0	0,0%		100,0%
Post test		100,0	0	0,0%		100,0%

	Kolmogorov-Smirnova			Shapiro-Wilk		
	Statistician	gl	Sig.	Statistician	gl	Sig.
Pre test	,159		,200*	,964		,833
Post test	,257		,028	,885		,102

*. This is a lower limit of true significance.

a. Lilliefors Significance correction

Normality		
P - value (Pre test) = 0.833		0,05
P - value (Post test) = 0.102		0,05
Conclusion: The data come from a normal distribution.		

STATISTICAL DECISION

Paired sample statistics

		Media	N	Deviation standard	Mean standard error
Par 1	Pre test	22,8333		2,03753	,58818
	Post test	29,5000		2,19504	,63365

		Matched differences						Sig.
	Media	Deviation standard	Mean standard error	95% confidence interval of the difference		t	gl	(bilateral)
				Inferior	Superior			
Par 1 Pre test - Post test	-6,66667	1,15470	,33333	-7,40033	-5,93300	-20,000		,000

Significance SPSS = 0.000	<	0,05

Conclusion: there is a significant difference between the pre-test and the post-test, so it is concluded that the running exercise test with thigh lifting does have significant effects on the improvement of child athletes.

In fact, athletes on average improved from 22.8333 points to 29.5000 points.

Thigh lift run with forward leg extension

NORMALITY

Kolmogorov - Smirnov: for large samples (> 30 individuals)

Shapiro - Wilk: small samples (< 30 individuals)

Criteria for determining normality:

Pre test => a = 0.05 Ho – The data come from a normal distribution.

Pos test < a = 0.05 H1 = Data **are** not from a normal distribution.

Case processing summary

	Cases					
	Valid		Lost		Total	
	N	Percentage	N	Percentage	N	Percentage
Pre test		100,0%	0	0,0%		100,0%
Post test		100,0%	0	0,0%		100,0%

Normality tests

	Kolmogorov-Smirnova			Shapiro-Wilk		
	Statistician	gl	Sig.	Statistician	gl	Sig.
Pre test	,123		,200*	,961		,800
Post test	,280		,010	,894		,133

*. This is a lower limit of true significance.

a. Lilliefors significance correction.

Normality

P - value (Pre test) = 0.800		0,05
P - value (Post test) = 0.133		0,05

Conclusion: The data come from a normal distribution.

STATISTICAL DECISION

Paired sample statistics

		Media	N	Deviation standard	Mean standard error
Par 1	Pre test	22,6667		2,46183	,71067
	Post test	29,3333		2,30940	,66667

	Matched differences								
			Mean standard error	95% confidence interval of the difference					Sig. (bilateral)
	Media	Deviation standard		Inferior	Superior	t	gl		
Par 1 Pre test - Post test	-6,66667	1,49747	,43228	-7,61812	-5,71522	-15,422			,000

Significance SPSS = 0.000	<	**0,05**
Conclusion: there is a significant difference between the pre-test and the post-test, so it is concluded that the running exercise test with thigh extension in front does have significant effects on the improvement of child athletes. In fact, athletes on average improved from 22.6667 points to 29.3333 points.		

Running with lower limb extension

NORMALITY

Kolmogorov - Smirnov: for large samples (> 30 individuals)

Shapiro - Wilk: small samples (< 30 individuals)

Criteria for determining normality:

Pre test => a = 0.05 Ho = The data come from a normal distribution.

Pos test < a = 0.05 H1 = Data **are** not from a normal distribution.

Case processing summary

	Cases					
	Valid		Lost		Total	
	N	Percentage	N	Percentage	N	Percentage
Pre test		100,0%	0	0,0%		100,0%
Post test		100,0%	0	0,0%		100,0%

Normality tests

	Kolmogorov-Smirnova			Shapiro-Wilk		
	Statistician	gl	Sig.	Statistician	Gl	Sig.
Pre test	,174		,200*	,954		,692
Post test	,272		,015	,828		,020

*. This is a lower limit of true significance.

a. Lilliefors significance correction.

Normality		
P - value (Pre test) = 0.692		0,05
P - value (Post test) = 0.020	<	0,05
Conclusion: The data come from a normal distribution.		

STATISTICAL DECISION

Paired sample statistics

		Media	N	Deviation standard	Mean standard error
Par 1	Pre test	24,1667		1,85047	,53418
	Post test	30,1667		1,69670	,48979

Paired samples test

	Matched differences							
				95% confidence interval of the difference				
	Media	Deviation standard	Mean standard error	Inferior	Superior	t	gl	Sig. (bilateral)
Par 1 Pre test - Post Test	-6,00000	,85280	,24618	-6,54185	-5,45815	-24,372		,000

Significance SPSS = 0.000	<	0,05

Conclusion: there is a significant difference between the pre-test and the post-test, so it is concluded that the Running with lower limbs extension exercise test does have significant effects on the improvement of child athletes. In fact, the athletes on average improved from 24.1667 points to 30.1667 points.

50 m race.

NORMALITY

Kolmogorov - Smirnov: for large samples (> 30 individuals)

Shapiro - Wilk: small samples (< 30 individuals)

Criteria for determining normality:

Pre test => a = 0.05 Ho = The data come from a normal distribution.

Pos test < a = 0.05 H1 = The data do not come from a normal distribution.

Case processing summary

	Cases					
	Valid		Lost		Total	
	N	Percentage	N	Percentage	N	Percentage
Pre test		100,0%	0	0,0%		100,0%
Post test		100,0%	0	0,0%		100,0%

Normality tests

	Kolmogorov-Smirnova			Shapiro-Wilk		
	Statistician	gl	Sig.	Statistician	gl	Sig.
Pre test	,272		,015	,903		,173
Post test	,291		,006	,867		,060

a. Lilliefors significance correction.

Normality		
P - value (Pre test) = 0.173		0,05
P - value (Pos test) = 0.060		0,05
Conclusion: The data come from a normal distribution.		

STATISTICAL DECISION

Paired sample statistics

	Media	N	Deviation standard	Mean standard error
Par 1 Pre test	25,5833		1,56428	,45157
Post test	30,5833		1,31137	,37856

Paired samples test

	Matched differences							
				95% confidence interval of the difference				
	Media	Deviation standard	Mean standard error	Inferior	Superior	t	gl	Sig. (bilateral)
Par 1Pre test - Post test	-5,00000	,95346	,27524	-5,60580	-4,39420	-18,166		,000

Significance SPSS = 0.000	<	0,05

Conclusion: there is a significant difference between the pre-test and the post-test, so it is concluded that the 50 m race exercise test does have significant effects on the improvement of child athletes.
In fact, athletes on average improved from 25.5833 points to 30.5833 points.

Discussion

After the analysis of the results of each of the tests performed, we were able to confirm that for the pre-test of the **thigh lifting run**, the results show that the technical performance of the thigh lifting run, the athletes analyzed presented very basic technical errors such as vision to the front, deficit in the support zone with the metatarsals, in maintaining the 90 degree angle in the swing and a deficit in the position of the hip and trunk, showing a lack of strength noted in those athletes, deficit in the support zone with the metatarsals, in the maintenance of the 90 degree angle in the swing and a deficit in the position of the hip and trunk, demonstrating a lack of strength noted in these muscle planes, on the other hand the results also showed that there is a marked emphasis on the work of the arms, After applying an exercise guide it was possible to improve the results of the second observation, the data being validated by the Shapiro-Will statistical test to determine the levels of reliability and by Student's t-test which proved that there is a significant difference between the pre-test and post-test, so it is concluded that the test of the exercise running with thigh lifting does have significant effects on the improvement of child athletes. In fact, the athletes on average improved from 22.8333 points to 29.5000 points. In the case of the **thigh lift running with leg extension**, the results show that for the technical performance, the analyzed athletes presented certain basic technical errors such as the braking angle that should be at 90 degrees and not go beyond the center line of the body, deficit in the position of the trunk and in the position of the hip, and certain technical errors in the support zone, and certain technical errors in the metatarsal support zone showing a lack of strength noted in these muscular planes. After applying an exercise guide, the results of the second observation could be improved and the data validated by the Shapiro-Will statistical test to determine the levels of reliability and by Student's t-test which proved that there is a significant difference between the pre-test and the post-test, Therefore, it is concluded that the exercise test of the thigh lifting run with front leg extension does have significant effects on the improvement of the child athletes; in fact, the athletes on average improved from 22.6667 points to 29.3333 points. In the case of **running with extension of the lower limbs**, the results show that for technical performance, the athletes analyzed presented certain basic technical errors such as the angle of braking, which should be at 90 degrees and should not go beyond the center line of the body, deficit in the opening of the hands, After applying an exercise guide, the results of the second observation were improved and the data were validated by the Shapiro-Will statistical test to determine the levels of reliability and by Student's t-test, which proved that there is a significant difference between the pre-test and the post-test, Therefore, it is concluded that the exercise test Run with extension of the lower extremities does have significant effects on the improvement of the child athletes, in fact, the athletes on average improved from 24.1667 points to 30.1667 points. In the case of the **50 m. race,** the results show that for technical performance, the athletes analyzed presented basic technical errors such as a deficit in the forward view, in maintaining the 90-degree angle in the breaststroke and not going beyond the center line of the body, deficit in the opening of the hands, position of the trunk demonstrating a lack of strength noticed in those muscular planes after applying an exercise guide it was possible to improve the results of the second observation being validated the data by means of the statistical test of Shapiro-Will to determine the levels of reliability and by means of Student's T which proved that there is a significant difference between the pre-test and the post-test, for which it is concluded that the test of the exercise of the 50 m. Run exercise if it has significant effects on the improvement of the exercise of the 50 m. run. In fact, the athletes on average improved from 25.5833 points to 30.5833 points.

In this way we can determine that thanks to the application of an exercise guide after the pre-test, if it helps significantly in the improvement of the running technique in child athletes this could be verified through the application of the post-test and thanks to the statistical verification based on the statistical test of Shapiro - Will and Student's t-test.

CHAPTER 4

CONCLUSIONS AND RECOMMENDATIONS

4.1 CONCLUSIONS

After the research was completed, the following conclusions were reached:

- When analyzing theoretical references according to the teaching-learning processes of the running technique in the discipline of athletics in the country, we realized that they are quite scarce, therefore, coaches have insufficient bases on how to impart an adequate practice regarding the improvement of the running technique to child athletes.

- The exercise guide, created with specific exercises in running technique, helped the athlete to develop this skill.

- The adjustments that were made to the practices for the improvement of the running technique were as expected, due to the fact that an improvement could be observed in the 5 weeks.

4.2 RECOMMENDATIONS

- To take into account theoretical references at the Latin American level that support the teaching-learning processes of the running technique in the discipline of athletics, so that in this way the coaches have adequate bases at the time of teaching a sport practice.

- It is recommended that the exercise guides have parameters aimed at an adequate development within the sports disciplines, so that the athlete can develop in the best way in the sport.

- The adaptations should always be carried out based on the development of practices according to the capacity to be improved in this case of the subject worked on the running technique in child athletes, and together with the help of a technical evaluation sheet.

BIBLIOGRAPHY

Brigaud, F. (2015). *Running, Posture, Biomechanics and Performance.* Badalona (Spain): Editorial Paidotribo.

Cevallos Camacho, T. (2014). *Sports initiation program in athletics to improve the teaching-learning processes in students of the Machachi Educational Unit, Mejia canton, province of Pichincha during the school year 2014 - 2015.* Latacunga.

Díaz Bordenave, J., & Martins Pereira, A. (1997). *Estrategias de ensenanza - aprendizaje.* San José: IICA.

RUNNING School. (December 5, 2019). Retrieved from Runner's Running Technique: What it is and how to improve: https://escueladerunning.com/tecnica-de- running/

García Cortina , G. (2018). *The self-structuring of knowledge based on forms of compression.* UNID Editorial Digital.

Hornillos Baz, I. (2000). *Atletismo.* Barcelona: INDE Publicaciones.

MOCHA-BONILLA, J. A. (2018). Effects of a recreational games program on laterality definition. Revista ESPACIOS, 39(23). *Revista ESPACIOS, 39(23),* 26.

Montoro, R. (2013). *Electronic book destined to the teaching of athletics in the process of basic sports training.* (L. d. Paz, Ed.) Havana: S/N.

Narváez Galván, E. F. (2014). *The pedagogical evaluation and its impact on competitive development in middle-distance events in prejuvenile athletes of the Sports Federation of Loja period 2013.* Loja.

Ortiz Ocana, A. L. (2009). *Pedagogical, didactic and methodological issues .* CEPEDID EDITIONS.

Romero Frometa, E., & Scrubb, M. E. (November 2003). efdeportes.*com.* Retrieved from La ensenanza de la técnica de las carreras en la etapa de iniciación: https://www.efdeportes.com/efd66/carreras.htm

Salas López, G. E. (2017). *The Teaching - Learning in the Technical Fundamentals of Table*

Tennis in High School students of the Educational Unit "Pedro Fermin Cevallos" of the canton Ambato province of Tungurahua. Ambato.

Sbert, A. (1969). *Métodos de Ensenanza en el Taller.* Bacelona: EDITORIAL REVERTE MEXICANA,S.A.

Sicilia Camacho, Á., & Delgado Noguera, M. Á. (2002). Physical Education and Teaching Styles. In *Análisis de la participación del alumnado desde un modelo socio-cultural del conocimiento escolar (*pp. 22-23). Barcelona: INDE Publicaciones.

Tobar, M. A., & Zurata, J. E. (2013). *Methodological guide for the improvement of running technique in long-distance athletes of the Trotahacheros Club of the Municipality of Tuquerres-Narino.* Santiago de Cali.

Vinuesa M., C. J. (1997). *Tratado de Atletismo.* Madrid: Editorial Esteban Sanz M.

ANNEXES

Graph 10 F.D.T. athletes in practices

Annex 2: Exercise guide for athletes.

EXERCISE GUIDE
TRAINING FOR THE DEVELOPMENT OF RUNNING TECHNIQUES

Objective: To optimize the running technique in flat races, in children athletes of the F.D.T., based on specific exercises for the development of this quality.

Running with thigh lift		
Variants		
Development of the exercise	**Graphical explanation**	**Methodological indications**
Materials: Track **Execution:** With only one lower limb raising the thigh and a 90° flexion of the other knee will be fully extended, they will advance 30 m. to the front, then change limbs and perform the same procedure. **Objective: To** mechanize the movement and position of the lower extremities in the running exercise with thigh raise.		- Smooth movement without excessive contraction of the muscle planes - Front view - Angle of 90° in the swing and not to go beyond the centerline of the body. - Semi-closed hands - Upright trunk - Raised hips - The elevated leg should be parallel to the ground with the knee bent at a 90° angle, toe facing forward. - Supporting leg fully extended and resting on the metatarsus.
Material: PLATENS **Execution: The** plates will be placed one next to the other at a distance of 1m, the athlete will jump over them at the order of execution, assimilating the exercise of lifting thighs. **Objective: To** achieve progress with thigh elevation with knee flexion at 90° degrees.		

Material: CONES or FENCES
Execution: The cones or hurdles will be placed one next to the other at a distance of 1m, the athlete will jump over them at the order of execution assimilating the exercise of thigh lifting.
Objective: To achieve progress with thigh elevation with knee flexion at 90° degrees.

Material: SIZE or TAPE
Execution: 10 squares are drawn on the floor with a distance of 1m, on command the athlete steps on each square with assimilation of the thigh lifting exercise.
Objective: To achieve progress with thigh elevation with knee flexion at 90° degrees.

Thigh lift run with front leg extension

Variants

Materials: Track

Execution: The athlete will move 20 to 30 m. to the front, raising only one lower limb by lifting the thigh and extending the leg to the front while the other will be fully extended. The athlete will then perform the same procedure changing limbs.

Objective: To mechanize the movement and position of the lower extremities.

Materials: Track

Execution: The athlete will move to the front, raising thighs with extension of the limbs to the front touching the tips of the toes with the fingertips.

Objective: To make the athlete raise his or her drive leg extensively.

Material: Track

Execution: The athlete will move from 20 to 30 m. in a straight line performing the exercise by raising thighs with extension of the legs in front, remaining parallel to the ground.

Objective: To achieve that the athlete raises, widely his or her impulse weight.

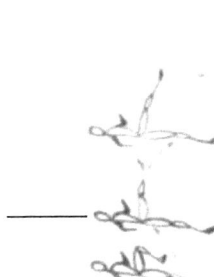

- Smooth movement without excessive contraction of the muscle planes

- Front view

- Angle of 90° in the swing and not to go beyond the centerline of the body.

- Semi-closed hands

- Upright trunk

- Raised hips

- The elevated leg then picked up will be extended and parallel to the ground with the toe of the foot slightly bent forward.

- Supporting leg extended and resting on the metatarsus.

Material: CONES or FENCES
Execution: The cones or hurdles will be placed one next to the other, on command the athlete will move laterally by the end of the hurdles raising thighs and extending legs for each one of them.
Objective: To get the athlete to extend his or her drive leg extensively.

Material: Track
Execution: The athlete has to perform the exercise in his own space after a set time, subsequently he will leave at speed to a signaled point.
Objective: To get the athlete to extend his or her drive leg extensively.

Running with lower limb extension

Variants

Materials: Track
Execution: The athlete will move 20 to 30 m. to the front, extending one of the limbs to the front while the other will move without extension to the front. The athlete will then perform the same procedure changing limbs.
Objective: To mechanize the movement and position of the lower extremities in running with extension of the lower extremities.

1. Smooth movement without excessive contraction of the muscle planes
2. Front view

		3. Angle of 90° in the swing and not to go beyond the centerline of the body. 4. Semi-closed hands 5. Upright trunk 6. High hips 7. The elevated leg shall be extended at a 45° angle to the other, the toe of the foot slightly bent forward. 8. Extended support leg and resting on the metatarsus.
Material: Track **Execution:** The athlete will perform the displacement at a distance of 20 to 30 m. performing the exercise with extension of the lower extremities. **Objective:** Rapid lowering of the lower extremities.		
Material: Chalk or Tape **Execution:** 12 squares are drawn on the floor one after the other, then the athlete has to step inside each of the squares performing the exercise extension of the lower extremities. **Objective:** Rapid lowering of the lower extremities.		
Material: Track, and tape. **Execution:** Athletes will move 5m to the front moving backwards 2m, they will repeat this until completing the distance of 30m. It is important to emphasize that they will perform the exercise with extension of the lower extremities when they move to the front, they will jog backwards with their backs turned. **Objective:** Rapid lowering of the lower extremities.		

50 m race.

Material: Track
Execution: The athlete at the order of the coach, will go out at speed performing the movements according to technique, it should be noted that it will move 50 m. to the front.
Objective: To evaluate the technical capacity of the athletes.
Variants: At the starting site they will be placed in different positions such as: dorsal cubitus, ventral cubitus, on their backs, sitting on the floor, squatting.

- The length of the stroke approach varies from 10 steps for beginners to more than 20 steps for high-level athletes.
- Running technique is similar to speed running.
- The speed increases continuously up to the take-off table.
- The last 3 steps are characterized by being long, longer. Short and fast.

Combined exercises

Materials: Track
Execution: the athlete will combine the running exercise with thigh lifting with the running exercise with extension of the lower limbs moving from 20 to 30 m.
Objective: Coordination between the lower extremities.

- Smooth movement without excessive contraction of the muscle planes
- Front view
- Angle of 90° in the swing and not to go beyond the centerline of the body.
- Semi-closed hands
- Upright trunk
- Raised hips

Materials: Track
Execution: The athlete will combine the running exercise lifting thighs with extension of the legs to the front with the running exercise with extension of the lower extremities.
Objective: Coordination between the lower extremities.

- The elevated leg then picked up will be extended and parallel to the ground with the toe of the foot slightly bent forward.
- Extended support leg resting on the metatarsus
- Coordination of movement.